Angelo Tartuferi

MICHELANGELO
painter, sculptor and architect

art courses

Introduction
by Antonio Paolucci

The Restoration of the Sistine Chapel Frescoes
by Fabrizio Mancinelli

ATS Italia Editrice

Summary

right:
Daniele da Volterra,
Bust of Michelangelo
Florence, Galleria dell'Accademia

Introduction

Michelangelo or the "sublime genius". It is virtually impossible for men and women of our generation to escape the awesome influence of a critical history that has conditioned us for centuries.

The adjective "sublime" (or the no less peremptory "terrible" or "divine") has been attributed to Michelangelo since the time of Ascanio Condivi and Giorgio Vasari, his contemporaries. In the opening words of the biography of Michelangelo Buonarroti in Vasari's "Lives" we read: "...the most benignant rector of Heaven cast his merciful eyes towards the earth and... decided to send into the world an artist who would be skilled in every art and craft, whose work would serve to show us how to achieve perfection in art – in drawing and in the use of contour, in using light and shadow to create relief in painting – and to use judgement in sculpture, and, in architecture, make dwellings safe, comfortable, healthy, pleasant, well-proportioned and rich in ornament. He determined, moreover, to give this artist a knowledge of true moral philosophy and the gift of poetry, so that the world might admire him and take him as a model in life, in work, in manners and in all human actions; so that he may be called divine rather than earthly". The process of deification has already taken place. The birth of Michelangelo is not a mere human birth, but an "epiphany", a divine manifestation. The imposition of his style is the epoch-making event that concludes – having reached a peak of perfection that will and can never be surpassed – the centuries old labour of the arts: Michelangelo is thus "divine rather than earthly". This is how he is described by Vasari. We are given a similar description by Ascanio Condivi, his favourite pupil, whose reverential admiration appears misted and softened by affection. His "Life" begins thus:"From the moment that God, in his beneficence, granted me the honour not only of enjoying the presence (into which I scarcely hoped to come), but also the affection, the conversation and the intimate friendship of that rare painter and sculptor, Michelangelo Buonarroti...". Condivi talks of his friendship with the artist in terms of a mystical experience, an ineffable privilege. From the beginning the myth of Michelangelo grew up around the idea of the unique, the extraordinary, the "other", as we see from this brief critical anthology: "I am so enthusiastic about Michelangelo that not even Nature can satisfy me after him, for I cannot see her with his eyes" (Goethe, Italian Journey); "The only sentiment that divinity can inspire in feeble mortals is terror: and Michelangelo seems born on purpose to stamp this fear in the soul..." (Stendhal, Roman Walk); "From the first moment Michelangelo was a total personality, almost frightening in his single-mindedness" (Wölfflin 1899). Michelangelo god or "titan". Thus, a critical idea that started with Vasari and Condivi, ably assisted by the artist himself during his lifetime with his absolutely exceptional existential and literary behaviour, has been handed down to us, influencing the thought and actions of millions of people. For a public from all over the world, Michelangelo represents today a "fatal attraction". No other artist of the past, neither Raphael nor Rembrandt or even Leonardo da Vinci enjoys such a vast, acritical and unconditioned consensus. And it is certainly not a coincidence that Michelangelo's sculpture-symbols (the "Pietà" in St. Peter's in Rome and the "David" in the Accademia in Florence) have been, in recent years, the victims of senseless vandalism. In a certain sense these episodes are the direct result of the myth. The "Stendhal syndrome" has shown its dark side. All this, if we consider it carefully, stems from the critical (and museographical) interpretation of Michelangelo that has historically been given. Take, for example, the present collocation of the "David" in its 19th century museum setting in the Accademia. The statue has an almost liturgical collocation as the altar of the Eucharist in a church; it stands, isolated in its awesome beauty, in the centre of the tribune-apse, in the zenithal light that comes from the skylight, like the tabernacle of the Holy Sacrament. Its image is immediately given a kind of secular consecration until it takes on, in the collective imagination, the propitiatory and ritual function of a divinity. Since the gods govern the absolute and the irrational, and since they are objects of love and (more rarely) hate, the logical consequence is the violent dialogue between the madman and the god – a god created by art historians. Are the criticisms directed against the restoration (moreover accurate) of the Sistine Chapel ceiling not the consequence of a critical myth that the cleaning has helped to put in crisis? We were used to thinking of Michelangelo in terms of black and white, the colours typical of the "terrible" or "sublime", and now, perhaps, we are disappointed by the bright, acid colours of the Mannerist palette, so close to Pontormo and Rosso and, thus, so firmly placed in historical perspective.

The point is that, when we face the question of Michelangelo, the real problem lies in overcoming the ahistorical or metahistorical tangent that for centuries has oriented the interpretation of his personality. The monograph that these lines introduce treats in an objectively concrete way, with supporting factual evidence, the stylistic development of one of the greatest protagonists in the history of art of all time. It is this kind of objectivity that we most need today.

Antonio Paolucci

The life of Michelangelo

Michelangelo was born on 6 March 1475, at Caprese in the Casentino between Arezzo and Chiusi, where his father, Lodovico di Leonardo Buonarroti (1446-1531) held the post of "podestà". The artist's mother was Francesca di Neri (1455-1481), a Florentine. In 1488 a young friend, the Florentine painter, Francesco Granacci (1469-1543) introduced Michelangelo to Domenico Ghirlandaio in whose important workshop he was given a three-year contract of apprenticeship. During this period he made copies of frescoes by Giotto and Masaccio (some drawings are in collections in Paris, Louvre; Munich, Staatliche Graphische Sammlung; Vienna, Albertina) and painted a panel (now lost) of the "Temptation of St. Anthony", inspired by an engraving by the German painter, Martin Schongauer (c. 1440-1494). Leaving Ghirlandaio's shop before the end of his contract, Michelangelo went in 1489 to work in the Medici gardens of the convent of San Marco in Florence where the sculptor, Bertoldo di Giovanni (c. 1440-1491), ran a school for young artists under the direct protection of Lorenzo the Magnificent and interested mainly in the study of classical sculpture. The young Michelangelo was invited by Lorenzo himself to reside in the Medici Palace, where he came into contact with the major figures of Florentine Humanism, including Agnolo Poliziano, Marsilio Ficino, the most important Platonic thinker – a philosophy in which Michelangelo maintained a firm belief throughout his life – and Cristoforo Landino, a scholar of Dante, whose poetry Michelangelo always loved. Michelangelo's first works in sculpture date from the early part of the last decade of the Quattrocento. In October 1494 the artist hurriedly left Florence which was about to be invaded by the army of Charles VIII. He went first to Bologna, then Venice, returning almost immediately to Bologna where he stayed for a year, working on the three sculptures for the tomb of St. Dominic in the church of the same name. During his first stay in Rome between 1496 and 1501, Michelangelo is recorded as having made a cartoon (now lost) for a painting of "St. Francis Receiving the Stigmata", destined for the church of St. Peter in Montorio but never painted. During this period he made the statue of "Bacchus", now in the Bargello in Florence and the "Pietà" in St. Peter's in the Vatican. When he returned to Florence in the spring of 1501, he was given numerous commissions for works of sculpture, including the "David", now in the Galleria dell'Accademia. In 1504 he was given the important commission of painting the fresco of the "Battle of Cascina", alongside Leonardo's "Battle of Anghiari" in the Council Chamber of Palazzo Vecchio in Florence. Three "tondi" also date from the first decade of the Cinquecento, two in sculpture and one painted on panel, known as the "Doni Tondo" (Florence, Uffizi). In March 1505 Julius II commissioned Michelangelo to make a project for his monumental tomb. This work was to prove a real 'tragedy' for the artist who successively abandoned the project and took it up again over the next forty years, finally only partially completing it.

Michelangelo's house at Caprese

In May 1508 work started on the frescoes for the Sistine Chapel ceiling. The total secrecy and solitude with which Michelangelo completed the work in October 1512 is perhaps the most typical aspect of the life of this extraodinary man, and totally different to that of the other artistic genius of early Cinquecento Rome, Raphael Sanzio, who exploited to a maximum the 'wordly' aspects of his work.

In the following years the artist worked mainly in Florence, where the Medici had returned to power in 1512, and where he completed to a greater or lesser extent his great architectural and sculptural projects: the facade of the church of San Lorenzo, the Laurentian Library, the Medici Chapel or New Sacristy in San Lorenzo. In 1530 he painted a "Leda" for Duke Alfonso d'Este of Ferrara, then giving it, however, to Antonio Mini who took it to France where it was lost. In the winter of 1532-33 Michelangelo was in Rome where he became friends with the nobleman Tommaso de' Cavalieri, a friend-ship that was to last until his death. The artist painted for him a series of mythological drawings (London, British Museum; Windsor, Royal Library). The cartoon of "Noli me tan-gere", made for Alfonso d'Avalos. also dates from the 1530s; the cartoon is now lost but we have copies by Bronzino and Pontormo, who also made a painting (Florence, Uffizi) from another cartoon, "Venus and Cupid" (1532-34).

In the spring of 1536 Michelangelo started work on the grandiose fresco of the "Last Judgement" on the altar wall of the Sistine Chapel; it was finished in November 1541. Shortly after Paul III commissioned the fres-coes for the Pauline Chapel in the Vatican, painted between 1542 and 1550. In his old age Michelangelo received much support, particularly spiritual, from his great friend-ship with the marchesa Vittoria Colonna (1490-1547), for whom he painted a "Christ crucified with mourners", now lost, but for which we have the preparatory drawing (London, British Museum).

"River god"
Florence, Casa Buonarroti

Study for "Hercules and Cacus"
Florence, Casa Buonarroti

Michelangelo continued to work up until a few days before his death on the "Rondanini Pietà" (Milan, Castello Sforzesco). He died on 18 February 1564, at about four thirty in the afternoon, after being in bed for only two days. His friend, Tommaso de' Cavalieri who "he loved more than any other" (Vasari) was with him, together with Daniele da Volterra and a few others. The body was taken to the church of Santi Apostoli; the Pope wanted him buried in St. Peter's but his nephew, Leonardo Buonarroti, had the body brought back to Florence where it arrived on March 10th and was buried in the church of Santa Croce. A memorial service was held on July 14th in the church of San Lorenzo.

FLORENCE

Casa Buonarroti

BATTLE OF THE CENTAURS AND LAPITHS
Marble. 82 x 91.5 cm

Early critics (Condivi, Vasari) both point to Angelo Poliziano (died 1494) as the source of inspiration for this classical theme that the 16-17 year-old Michelangelo realized in a sculpture of extraordinary technical and expressive maturity.
We also know from Condivi that Michelangelo was unusually pleased with this work that he kept with him throughout his life. Art historians have long debated the exact iconographical explanation of the relief. Over and above the narrative description of the episode, however, the artist seems most interested in the infinite variety of light and form offered by the tangle of nude figures. The work's reference to the front panels of sarcophagi of imperial Rome has always been emphasized, but a credible hypothesis also points to the influence of the works of classical inspiration created by artists in the second half of the 13th century, particularly Nicola Pisano.

MADONNA OF THE STEPS
Marble. 57 x 40 cm

The first and most important critical reference to this marble relief made by Michelangelo at the age of about 15, was Giorgio Vasari's (1568): "wishing to copy the style of Donatello, he did it so well that the work seems to be by Donatello, except that here there is more grace and design". More generally, we can say that Michelangelo's first masterpiece is a brilliant interpretation not only of Donatello's art but of the figurative tradition of the early Renaissance and in particular of the painting of Masaccio. Moreover, Michelangelo's interest in the art of earlier periods is shown in his beautiful drawings of Giotto's frescoes in the Peruzzi Chapel in Santa Croce in Florence (Paris, Louvre). In the figures of the "putti" climbing the staircase we already see Michelangelo's use of the "nonfinito", possibly derived from Donatello and yet interpreted in a very different, purely sculptural way, with no attempt to imitate or integrate the expressive possibilities of painting that characterize the work of the great sculptor of the early Quattrocento.

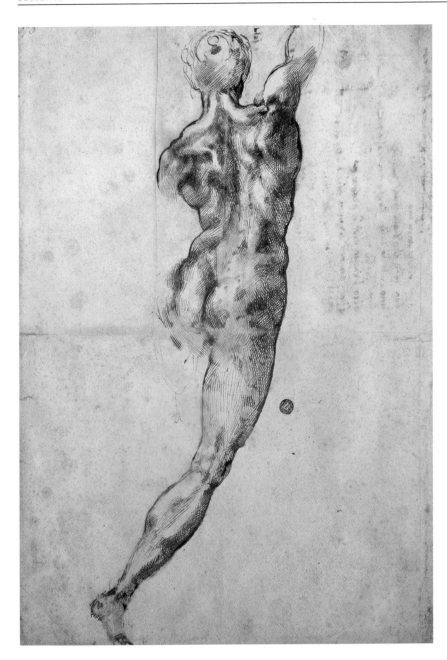

STUDY OF NUDE FIGURE FOR THE BATTLE OF CASCINA
Drawing in pen with black pencil.
40.8 x 28.4 cm

This is undoubtedly one of Michelangelo's most famous drawings,
traditionally referred to the lost cartoon for the "Battle of Cascina".
It is one of the most "polished" of the drawings that can be attributed
to the artist and critics have noted that in his handling of graphic
work, too, Michelangelo attempted to interpret the material in successive layers. It is difficult to define the strength that runs through
the line of the figure from the contour of the foot to the unfinished
raised right arm.

MODEL FOR THE FAÇADE OF THE CHURCH OF SAN LORENZO IN FLORENCE
Wood, 217 x 285 cm

Generally considered, particularly in the past, to be the model that
Michelangelo had made by Baccio d'Agnolo in 1516-17 from his original drawing but then harshly rejected once it was finished. According to de Tolnay, however, it is the second model, prepared by the artist together with Pietro Urbano, who took it to Rome on 22 December
1517. This final model, once kept in San Lorenzo itself, corresponds
to the drawing no. 43 A in Casa Buonarroti and more exactly fits the
description given in the contract for the construction of the façade of
the church, drawn up on 19 January 1518 and then cancelled on 10
March 1520.

PLAN FOR THE CHURCH OF
SAN GIOVANNI DEI FIORENTINI IN ROME
Drawing in pencil, pen and wash, 41.6 x 37.2 cm

Michelangelo's interest in the project for
the church of San Giovanni dei Fiorentini is
attested by the three plans in Casa Buonarroti and the artist's correspondence with Cosimo I de' Medici, who expressed his enthusiastic approval in a letter of 30 April 1560: "your
design for the church of the Nation so pleased
us that we regret not seeing the completed
work that will honour and glorify our city and
also your name".

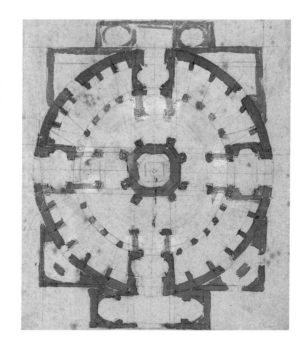

STUDY FOR THE LAST JUDGEMENT
IN THE SISTINE CHAPEL
Charcoal and pen, 41.5 x 29.8 cm

Condivi (1553) states that Michelangelo sub-
mitted the project for the fresco of the Last
Judgement in the Sistine Chapel to Clement VII just before the Pope's death in September 1534. Paul III fully backed the project
which, however, was only started in November 1536. The study in Casa Buonarroti is one
of Michelangelo's most important composi-
tional drawings and most probably quite close
to the definitive plan for the work mentioned
by Condivi.

Santo Spirito

CRUCIFIX
Wood, ht. 135 cm

"He made a wooden Crucifix for the church of Santo Spirito in Florence and it was placed above the lunette of the high altar where it is now" (Vasari). Considered lost for a very long time, it was recognized and identified as a work by Michelangelo in 1962 by M.Lisner, who dated the work to October 1494, before the artist's night to Bologna. It is the earliest work in full relief that we have by Michelangelo who made it at the age of nineteen. The inscription on the tablet at the top is taken from the Gospel of St. John: "Jesus, of Nazareth, King of the Jews", and is written in Hebrew, Greek and Latin. The words are written from right to left, which may be explained by the fact that Michelangelo was left-handed. In the gentle curves of the body – very different to Michelangelo's 'terrible' later style – critics have identified the influence of Leonardo.

Bargello National Museum

MADONNA AND CHILD ("PITTI TONDO")
Marble, max. ht. 85.5 cm

This work, made in about 1504-5 for Bartolomeo Pitti, was a private commission, evident in the intimacy of the tone. There is a preparatory drawing for the relief in the Musée Condé at Chantilly.

BACCHUS
Marble, ht. 184 cm (without the base)

The strange ambivalence of the sculpture was already clear to Michelangelo's contemporaries; Vasari notes "a harmony of wonderful elements... the slenderness of a youth and the rounded fullness of the female form". Carved during the artist's first stay in Rome and, according to most critics, probably before (1496-97) the "Pietà" in the Vatican, for the banker, Jacopo Galli, a keen collector of antique sculpture and a great friend of Michelangelo. It was brought to Florence following the purchase by Francesco I de' Medici in 1571-72 and was moved to the Bargello in 1873.

BRUTUS
Marble, ht. 95 cm

According to Vasari (1568) Michelangelo entrusted the completion of
the bust of "Brutus"to his great friend and assistant, Tiberio Calcagni
(1532-1565). The work, inspired by the writer and good friend of the
artist. Donato Giannotti (1494-1563), was made for Cardinal Niccolò
Ridolfi. It is thought that Michelangelo intended the work to com-
memorate Lorenzino de' Medici, the new Brutus, who in January 1537
stabbed to death the hated Alessandro de' Medici, despotic ruler of the
city from 1532. The very great sense of classical antiquity that pervades
the marble is to be seen in relation to the source used by Michelangelo, as affirmed by Vasari: "a portrait of Brutus cut in cornelian... of great
antiquity".

DAVID-APOLLO
Marble, ht.146 cm (with the base)

Identified either as David – according to the entry in the inventory of the Grand Duke Cosimo I de' Medici (1553) – or, more
correctly, as Apollo, according to Vasari, who records the work as
being made in about 1531 for Baccio Valori, Papal Governor of
Florence. According to de Tolnay, Michelangelo probably started the work in 1525-6, intending it to be a figure of David, but
then decided to change it into Apollo. Some scholars have rather
unconvincingly linked the statue to the sculptures for the Medici
Chapel in San Lorenzo; the marble does, however, bear an affinity
to these works in its subtle sense of psychological unease.

Galleria dell'Accademia

DAVID
Marble, ht. 410 cm

This sculpture was created out of a block of marble that had previously been worked, without success, by two Florentine sculptors: Agostino di Duccio (1418-c.1481) in 1462-63 and Antonio Rossellino (1427-c.l478) in 1476. The contract for the execution of the work was drawn up between Michelangelo and the "Operai" of Florence Cathedral on 16 August 1501 and stipulated a payment of 400 ducats. The artist worked on the sculpture over the next two years. On 25 January 1504, when the statue was almost finished, a commission made up of the major artists of the time – including Leonardo da Vinci, Botticelli, Filippino Lippi and Perugino – decided to place it, as a symbol of liberty and independence, outside the entrance to Palazzo Vecchio, seat of the Florentine civic government. At the beginning of September of the same year the statue was erected in the designated place. The "David" was moved to the Accademia in 1873 and in 1910 a marble copy was placed outside the entrance to Palazzo Vecchio. Vasari – who jealously guarded some fragments of the statue's arm, broken in the riots leading to the expulsion of the Medici in 1527 and replaced in 1543 – dedicates words of glowing praise and veneration to the work: "For in it the legs are beautifully drawn... such grace of pose has never again been seen... whoever has seen this, need see no other sculpture made now or at any other time by any other artist". Over the centuries the sculpture has become one of the universal symbols of art history of all time, that is every year admired, with greater or lesser awareness and motivation, by crowds of visitors from all over the world. This point leads us to the consideration of the problematics of the so-called modern phenomenon of mass culture, to which we must unfortunately link the recent episode of damage caused to the "David".

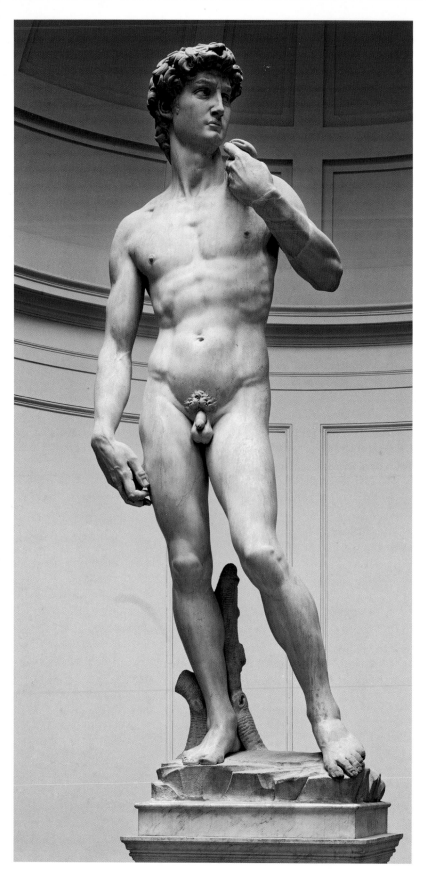

"David"
front view of the statue

St. Matthew
Marble, ht. 271 cm

In a contract drawn up on 24 April 1503 with the Arte della Lana, the Wool Merchants' Guild, Michelangelo was to make 12 statues of the Apostles for the Cathedral of Santa Maria del Fiore in Florence. However, the artist only executed this statue, which he worked on between 1505 and 1506, leaving it unfinished, while the contract was cancelled on 18 December 1505. The sculpture was moved from the Opera del Duomo to its present location in 1834. The crushed form of the marble block makes the work appear closer to a relief than a free-standing sculpture. In the particular contrapposto of the planes of the shoulders and the head critics have pointed to a reference to the famous fragment of Roman sculpture of the Hellenistic period, popularly known as "Pasquino".

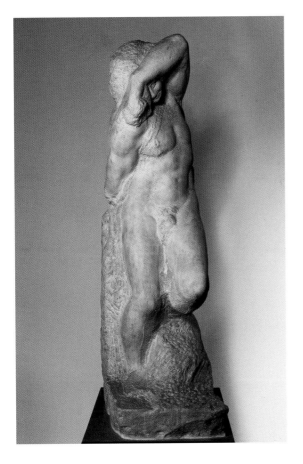

YOUNG SLAVE
Marble, ht. 256 cm

AWAKENING SLAVE
Marble, ht. 267 cm

Among the most famous of Michelangelo's sculptures, the four Captives or Slaves in the Accademia were made for the tomb of Pope Julius II, commissioned in 1505. As we know, the tomb finally built, now in the church of San Pietro in Vincoli in Rome, is very different from Michelangelo's grandiose conception of the project that he worked on over a period of forty years. These sculptures are generally dated to the early 1530s before Michelangelo's definitive departure for Rome in 1534. The Slaves were given to Grand Duke Cosimo I de' Medici by Leonardo Buonarroti, the artist's nephew, in 1564. They were placed in the Grotta del Buontalenti in the Boboli Gardens and moved to the Accademia in 1909. These statues exemplify more than any other work by Michelangelo the quality of suggestion implied in the unfinished work and have been particularly studied by scholars in an attempt to clarify the sculptor's methods of working.

The exact collocation of the Slaves on the tomb of Julius II is still not certain, but they were most probably destined to occupy the lower part of the monument, acting as a support for the upper orders: "These captives were all the provinces subjugated by this Pope and made obedient to the Catholic Church" (Vasari). This sculpture suggests more strongly than the others the struggle of the figure to free itself from the rough stone that seems to oppress it. The extraordinary strength of the muscles of the torso is remarkable in a sculpture.

BEARDED SLAVE
Marble, ht. 263 cm

This is the most finished of the sculptures and represents an older male figure. The melancholy look of the figure is often compared to the personification of "Dusk" in the Medici Chapel in San Lorenzo.

SLAVE KNOWN AS ATLAS
Marble, ht. 277 cm

This figure is hardly more than sketched in, given that only the left side is drawn in any depth. The extraordinary historical success of these sculptures has never waned, even in the 17th-18th century, when their unfinished state was recognized as a positive and 'modern' value, exactly as it is at the present time.

PIETÀ KNOWN AS THE PALESTRINA PIETÀ
Marble, ht. 253 cm

The statue comes from a chapel owned by the Barberini family at
Palestrina and was purchased by the Italian State in 1939. Unlike
other works by Michelangelo there is no reference to this work
in documents or contemporary critical writings; the first attribution to the artist dates from the first half of the 18th century.
It is certainly one of the most problematic works ascribable to
Michelangelo or his circle. The marble is an antique block that
had already been used as part of the architectural decoration.
Apart from some evident incongruences in the proportions, that
have always been pointed out by critics, the work seems to be too
obviously Michelangelesque to be entirely authentic.

The Uffizi Gallery

left:
HOLY FAMILY WITH ST. JOHN ("DONI TONDO")
Paint on panel, 120 cm diameter
(172 cm with cornice)

STUDY OF FIGURES
Black pencil and silverpoint, 23.5 x 35.6 cm

This work was commissioned by Agnolo Doni, probably on the occasion of his marriage to Maddalena Strozzi in January 1504, a hypothesis that would seem to be confirmed by the presence of the coat of arms of the Strozzi family in the beautifully carved cornice, with five heads in relief, attributed to Baccio da Montelupo. More recent critical opinion, however, tends to date the work a little later, suggesting it was painted at about the same time as the frescoes of the Sistine Chapel ceiling (1508-12). The work clearly draws inspiration from Hellenistic sculpture, particularly evident in the mysterious nude figures in the background. The extreme formal rigour of the painting was harshly criticized at the end of the 19th century when Jacob Burckhardt made his famous comment: "nobody should paint a Holy Family with feelings like this". The restoration carried out in 1984-5, which essentially entailed the precise and accurate cleaning of the painting, has revealed the supreme mastery of line, composition and also colour in the work. This is the only panel painting to be universally attributed to Michelangelo. It is a perfect example of Michelangelo's theory of painting put into practice: "I consider painting to be better the more it tends towards relief. It became part of the Medici collection in 1594 and in 1635 was placed in the Tribune of the Uffizi which housed the most prestigious works.

The attribution of this drawing, unfortunately in a poor state of conservation, to Michelangelo is generally accepted by the critics, who have always referred it to the lost cartoon of the "Battle of Cascina" that Michelangelo was to fresco in the Great Council Chamber in Palazzo Vecchio in Florence. The drawing is usually compared to the monochrome painting in the Earl of Leicester's Collection in Holkham Hall (Norfolk), attributed to Aristotile da Sangallo (1481-1551) and thought to be the most faithful copy of the lost cartoon by Michelangelo. The cartoon (1504-5) immediately became the object of passionate, almost fanatic study by a whole generation of artists, only to disappear into thin air after being transferred to Palazzo Medici, where it was perhaps broken up into several parts by enthusiastic followers. The subject of the lost cartoon was a historical episode of 1364, narrated in Villani's 14th century "Cronaca" of the war between the Florentines and Pisa. However, as in the early relief of the "Battle of the Centaurs" in Casa Buonarroti, the historical event is used mainly as an excuse for an inventive entanglement of nude bodies with finely drawn anatomies, confirming once more the primacy of drawing in all Florentine Renaissance art.

San Lorenzo

VIEW OF THE NEW SACRISTY

The first reference to Michelangelo's project for the New Sacristy dates from November 1520. In March 1521 the work was already underway and by the beginning of 1524 the cupola was finished. The original project was for a free-standing edifice that was to house four tombs – those of Lorenzo the Magnificent and his brother, Giuliano, and that of Giuliano, Duke of Nemours (died 1516) and son of Lorenzo the Magnificent, together with that of his nephew Lorenzo, Duke of Urbino (died 1519). The tombs of the two Medici popes, Leo X and Clement VII were to be added to these. In its realization, however, the project was limited to the tombs of the Dukes, while the remains of Lorenzo the Magnificent and his brother were placed below the statues of the "Madonna and Child" with "St. Cosmas" (made in 1531 by Giovanni Angelo di Michele known as Montorsoli, c. 1507-1563) and "St. Damian" (by Raffaello da Montelupo, 1505-C.1566), opposite the altar wall. Michelangelo made the sculptures for the chapel over a period of ten years between 1524-34.

THE NEW SACRISTY: VIEW OF THE VAULT

The hemispherical dome with its coffered decoration in perspective recalls that of the Pantheon but has a soaring lantern at the top, which plays a fundamental role in the lighting of the building. The similarity with the Old Sacristy by Filippo Brunelleschi (1377-1446) has always been emphasized; the grey and white of the "pietra serena" pillars against the white walls, the rectangular apse, the idea of the tabernacles above the doors and other elements derive, in fact, from Brunelleschi's architecture. However, Michelangelo's way of working was to start from certain traditional standpoints, then gradually distort them in terms of the accepted Renaissance canons: "he departed a great deal from what was regulated by proportion, order and rule, according to common usage and following Vitruvius and the works of antiquity" (Vasari).

TOMBS OF GIULIANO AND LORENZO DE' MEDICI

The two funeral monuments represent a complete break with the traditional iconography and structure of this particular genre. The artist's innovative impetus is strongly evident in every aspect of the decoration, from the capitals to the cornices, from the pilasters to the finest detail of the moulding. The motif of the two volutes on the curved top of each sarcophagus is given a strong sense of movement by the dynamic contrapposto of the four allegorical figures resting on them. The pyramidal conception of the whole was to have been completed at the base by the statues of the river gods, planned but never made.

above:
NIGHT AND DAY
Marble,
length 194 and 205 cm respectively

The two personifications of "Day" and "Night" are placed in a most natural-seeming position of terrible precariousness on the sarcophagus of Giuliano, Duke of Nemours. The female representation of "Night" is a highly polished figure that nevertheless seems to escape any kind of naturalistic or academic interpretation, while more authentic naturalistic notes are to he found in the owl beneath her leg or in the mask at her shoulder. In the figure of "Day" we note the contrast between the powerful, well-defined muscles of the body and the indistinct features of the face in the barely drawn in head.

below:
DUSK AND DAWN
Marble,
length 195 and 203 cm respectivily

The two sculptures rest on the sarcophagus of Lorenzo, Duke of Urbino. The impressive head of "Dusk" is again little more than suggested and is turned towards the sepulchre, while the more polished form of "Dawn" is caught in a moment of languid awakening.

GIULIANO DE' MEDICI, DUKE OF NEMOURS
Marble, ht. 173 cm

If the composition is reminiscent of that of
"Moses" in San Pietro in Vincoli in Rome, the
proud stance of the figure recalls the inherent
heroism of the "David" in the Accademia.

left:
MADONNA AND CHILD
Marble, ht. 226 cm

The twisting "contrapposto" gives the impression
of figures spinning in space, a theme that was to
become popular in Mannerist sculpture. In the
face of the Madonna, however, we see a return to
the search for an ideal, elevated form of beauty.

LORENZO DE' MEDICI, DUKE OF URBINO
Marble, ht. 178 cm

"The pensive Duke Lorenzo, the embodiment of
wisdom, with such fibely modelled legs that the
eye could see no better" (Vasari). This extraordinarily beautiful sculputure has also been interpreted as an allegorical representation of the contemplative life. In 1988-89 the cleaning of the
monument was undertaken by the Soprintenden-
za per I Beni Artistici e Storici of Florence.

LAURENTIAN LIBRARY:
'RICETTO' AND READING ROOM

"The Laurentian Library is one of Michelangelo's richest and most fully achieved architectural works" (P. Portoghesi, 1964). When Giulio de' Medici was elected Pope Clement VII (19 November 1523), Michelangelo was in Rome and must have received the commission for the new library to house the massive patrimony collected by the Medici directly from the new Pope. The artist accepted reluctantly, emphasizing as on other occasions the 'incompetence' of a sculptor: "I'll do what I can, although it is not my profession". The first drawings date from the beginning of 1524 and work must have gone ahead swiftly under the supervision of Nanni di Baccio Bigio, given that Michelangelo was also working at the same time on the sculptures for the adjacent New Sacristy in San Lorenzo. However, when the artist left definitively for Rome (1534), the library was still unfinished. The wonderful staircase leading from the 'ricetto' or vestibule to the reading room was completed in about 1556 by Bartolomeo Ammannati (1511-1592), who remained relatively faithful to Michelangelo's plans. As well as to the flowing spread of the three flights of the staircase, the visitor's eye is immediately drawn to the striking architectural design of the walls, divided up by pairs of columns sunk into the structure, the two equal superimposed orders giving an impression of vertical thrust. In contrast, the spatial tensions of the airy reading room are projected horizontally and the light enters in a continuous flow thanks to the uninterrupted sequence of windows on either side. The splendid wooden ceiling was made according to Michelangelo's design in 1550 by the specialists Battista del Tasso (1500-1555) and Antonio di Marco known as il Carota (1485-1568). The floor was completed between 1549 and 1554 by Santi Buglioni (1494-1576) and Niccolò Tribolo (c. 1500-1550), who also designed it. In antithesis to the dramatic contrasts of light and form in the 'ricetto', the reading room emanates a sense of intellectual quiet, coming from the only fully defined achievement of the architectural genius of Michelangelo.

Palazzo Vecchio

VICTORY
Marble, ht. 261 cm

This statue has been described as "the most enigmatic work Michelangelo left to posterity" (Justi). This statement encapsulates the many interrogatives still posed by this extraordinary work of sculpture. It is generally thought to have been made for the tomb of Julius II, but another hypothesis suggests that it was originally destined for the façade of San Lorenzo in Florence. The interpretation of the subject has also given rise to debate among scholars: the work has been seen as a political allegory alluding to the loss of freedom of the city of Florence or, alternatively, as a representation of platonic love.
Probably made in the early 1530s, the sculpture was acquired after the death of Michelangelo by Daniele da Volterra (c. 1509-1566), who in vain suggested placing it on Michelangelo's tomb.

Museum of the Opera del Duomo

right:
PIETÀ
Marble, ht. 226 cm

The work was begun in about 1548 and we learn from Vasari that in about 1555 the artist was working on it "almost everyday as a hobby" and that he wanted it placed over his tomb. At a certain point the block of marble, that had caused a great deal of problems from the beginning, broke and Michelangelo gave the surviving pieces to his great friend, Francesco Bandini, the Florentine sculptor and architect who died in 1564. Tiberio Calcagni (1532-1565) was convinced to reconstruct the group. As Vasari himself noted the 'unfinished' characterized Michelangelo's later period, influenced by an intense creative spirit, matched by an equally intense spiritual passion that led the artist to meditate on the theme of death almost to the point of obsession.

VATICAN
St. Peter's Basilica

PIETÀ
Marble, ht. 174 cm

The statue was commissioned by Cardinal Jean de Villiers de la Groslaye (died 1499), Charles VIII's ambassador to Pope Alexander VI. The contract for the work was drawn up on 27 August 1498 and stipulated a payment of 450 ducats. The work was completed by the end of the century. In this masterpiece of Michelangelo's early period, the theme of the lament for the dead Christ is interpreted in a way that is unusual within the Italian figurative tradition but, rather, inspired by Northern European iconographical models. In its realization, however, the work has nothing of the harsh naturalism and spiritual torment so dear to Northern artists. The artist's intention here would seem to be to make the sublime quality of divine beauty perceptible to human eyes. Giorgio Vasari (1511-1574), who is undoubtedly one of the greatest critics of all time of Michelangelo's work, also emphasizes in his Life of Michelangelo the purely technical aspect of the work: "that, in truth, one cannot but wonder how the hand of the artist could in so short a time and so perfectly have made such a divine work; it is indeed a miracle that a formless block of stone should be shaped to a perfection that nature herself is scarcely able to create in flesh". The artist himself must also have been aware of this extraordinary technical prowess, achieved at the age of twenty-three, and for the first and only time he signed his work, inscribing his name on the sash across the Madonna's breast. The sculpture was originally placed in the Chapel of St. Petronilla in the old basilica of St. Peter; when this was demolished in about 1535, it was moved to the Chapel of the Madonna della Febbre in the new church and in 1749 moved to the Chapel of the Crucifix (or of the Pietà).

THE DOME

Following the death of the architect, Antonio da Sangallo the Younger (1483-1546), Michelangelo found himself "with great dismay" having to take on responsibility for the Fabbrica di Palazzo Farnese, the Vatican fortifications and above all the Fabbrica di San Pietro. One of his main concerns for St. Peter's was to get back to the original plan for the construction of the basilica drawn up by Donato Bramante (1444-1514). Michelangelo did not hesitate to re-use on the exterior the "giant" order of composite pilasters that characterizes the internal structure of the basilica, thus reproducing the spatial unity devised by Bramante for the interior. Between 1559 and 1561 the great drum of the dome was completed as far as the top cornice. However, death prevented Michelangelo from completing his projects and above all from constructing the great dome. We nevertheless have an idea of his intentions thanks mostly to three engravings by Etienne Duperac, published in 1569, showing the plan, elevation and cross-section of the south side of the basilica, coming almost certainly from the last model prepared by Michelangelo. From these engravings and, more decisively, from signed drawings in the Teyler Museum in Haarlem (no. A29 r.) and in the Wicar Collection of the Musée des Beaux-Arts in Lille (no. 93 r.), it is clear that the artist envisaged a great dome consisting of two superimposed hemispherical shells.

In 1573-74 the architect Giacomo della Porta (1540-1602) was named chief architect of St. Peter's, and the dome was finally constructed between 1588 and 1590, while the lantern was added by 1593. The lantern is faithful to Michelangelo's original plan, while the internal shell and more particularly the external one are considerable raised.

MODEL FOR THE DOME OF ST. PETER'S
Wood, 530 x 480 cm

This great lime wood model for the dome is generally thought to be that made by a group of woodworkers under the direction of Michelangelo between November 1558 and 9 November 1561. The most widely supported hypothesis suggests that Giacomo della Porta worked directly on the model, having a new external shell built by the Florentine sculptor, Taddeo Landini, thus substantially modifying the external profile of the dome which is much higher than in Michelangelo's original idea. The lantern, on the other hand, most probably respects the original project. In the model the great windows of the drum have triangular pediments whereas in fact Michelangelo built them alternately with triangular and curved pediments.

DELPHICA

The Sistine Chapel

THE DECORATION OF THE SISTINE CHAPEL

The great chapel of the Vatican palace, dedicated to Our Lady of the Assumption and generally known as the Sistine Chapel, was built by the Florentine architect, Giovanni de' Dolci at the start of the last quarter of the 15th century for Pope Sixtus IV (Francesco Della Rovere, 1414-1484). Between 1480 and 1483 the side walls were decorated by the most important Tuscan and Umbrian artists of the time – including Botticelli, Domenico Ghirlandaio, Luca Signorelli, Perugino and Pintoricchio – while the ceiling was painted blue all over and decorated with gold stars by Pier Matteo d'Amelia, a painter from Umbria. We know that Michelangelo was contacted by Julius II about the decoration of the ceiling as early as May 1506, while work did not start until 10 May 1508. In these two years the artist was obviously convinced to overcome his initial reluctance to accept the commission, documented by contemporary sources and motivated above all by his often repeated declarations of technical incompetence outside the field of sculpture. In a famous letter written to his father in January 1509, when the work had already been underway for several months, Michelangelo wrote: "my work is not going ahead as I think it should: and this is the problem, for it is not my profession". The first problem Michelangelo was faced with was that of building the scaffolding that would enable him to work safely at a height of over twenty metres. Documentary sources (Condivi, Vasari) give a detailed account of this preparatory stage of the work; the technique adopted was similar to that used in the construction of vaulted ceilings; tiered structures were erected on "props" (protruding from the walls) at the sides of six windows of the chapel. Michelangelo first built three of these tiered structures, and linked them together solidly with movable planks in order to paint the first half of the work that was unveiled on 15 August 1511. The same procedure was then repeated for the second part of the work. In the original project for the decoration drawn up by Michelangelo, probably according to the wishes of Julius II, the twelve Apostles were depicted surrounded by a decoration in 'grotesque'. But once the artist was given a free hand, he invented an incredible illusionistic architectural structure that served as a framework for the progressive realization of the divine Revelation and Redemption. Iconographically the work is divided into three parts. The first part is made up of the fourteen lunettes at the top of the walls of the chapel with the eight triangular spandrels of the vault depicting figures from the Old Testament, chiefly the Ancestors of Christ. In the pendentives where the walls join the ceiling at the four corners are scenes of "Judith and Holofernes" and "David and Goliath" (above the entrance); "the Punishment of Haman" and "The Brazen Serpent" (above the altar wall). The second and third parts are the vault itself. A cornice is formed of monumental marble thrones with seven Prophets and five Sibyls heralding the coming of Christ. The central rectangle is divided into nine sections by painted architectural ribs coming from the plinths of the thrones, on which ten pairs of nude youths sit. Between the figures in each pair is a medallion, painted in monochrome to look like gilded bronze and depicting a scene from the Old Testament. In the nine central sections are scenes from the book of Genesis, running in chronological order from the altar towards the entrance wall: "God separating light from darkness"; "The creation of heaven and earth"; "God separating the waters from the land"; "The creation of man"; "The creation of woman"; "The Fall" and "The Expulsion from Paradise"; "The sacrifice of Noah"; "The Deluge"; "The drunkenness of Noah". The names of the Florentine artists who assisted Michelangelo, under his strict supervision, during the initial stages of the work are also well known. The most important was Francesco Granacci (c. 1469-1543), his childhood friend who had introduced him to the workshop of Ghirlandaio in Florence; others from Ghirlandaio's workshop were Giuliano Bugiardini (1475-1556) and Jacopo di Sandro (known 1500-1554), who was substituted in January 1509 because of a disagreement with Michelangelo by Jacopo di Lazzaro di Pietro Torni, known as Indaco Vecchio (1476-1526). Other assistants were Agnolo di Donnino, known as Mazziere (1466-1513)

and Aristotile da Sangallo (1481-1551), nephew of the famous Giuliano da Sangallo, a life-long friend of Michelangelo. Two little known artists from Emilia, Giovanni Trignoli and Bernardino Zacchetti (1472-c. 1525) are also recorded as having worked there in 1510. From the end of 1509, however, most of the Florentine painters had to leave the Sistine scaffolding and Michelangelo was left to finish the work practically by himself, helped only by a few apprentices on the secondary parts – the architectural framework, the "tondi" and the "putti" on the thrones of the Prophets. Following the unveiling of the first part of the ceiling, Michelangelo was received on 30 September 1511 by the Pope, who gave him the 500 ducats stipulated in the contract for the continuation of the painting. A year later the work was finished, with a physical commitment on the part of the artist that is still amazing today. Restoration of the frescoes was begun in June 1980 under the direction of Fabrizio Mancinelli and carried out by the

Vatican restorers, led by Gianluigi Colalucci. In October 1984 the cleaning of the fourteen lunettes was completed, while in December 1989 restoration started on the "Last Judgement"; this was completed in 1994. It is not easy to adequately express the significance of the restoration of the Sistine Chapel frescoes, the historical importance of which will probably only become evident with the passing of time. The scrupulously controlled removal of the layer of dirt, as well as the retouching and repainting, that had covered the painting for centuries, has made us the privileged witnesses to the renewal of Michelangelo's masterpiece that we now see, at the turn of this century, in a completely new way and – far more importantly – certainly much closer to the way in which his contemporaries saw it. In contrast to his alleged technical incapacity, referred to at the beginning, the restoration has revealed the artist's complete mastery of mural painting, in the wake of the best Tuscan tradition from Giotto to Masaccio.

The plaster is amazingly uniform, showing that there was little need for the finishing touches to be added "a secco", according to the classic rules of "buon fresco". The application of colour is particularly interesting, characterized by a 'liquid' colour, applied in successive layers of glazing that gives the painted surface a delicacy and transparency as well as an extraordinary luminosity, that can be appreciated from the ground but which appears truly remarkable to those who have had the fortune to see it closely from the scaffolding erected for the restoration work; personally, I keep a vivid impression of this experience. There is no doubt that the revelation of "Michelangelo's great luminosity" (P. Rotondi) is the most important achievement of this restoration and that most immediately visible to the observer.

THE CREATION OF THE STARS AND THE PLANTS

Cleaning has restored the luminosity of the right hand side of the painting with God creating the sun and the moon. On the left the bold figure of the Eternal Father is shown in the act of creating the vegetation on Earth.

left:
THE SEPARATION OF LIGHT FROM DARKNESS

This image, representing a totally new pictorial image, is one of the last parts of the ceiling to be painted. Frescoed in a single 'day's work' the scene is striking both for the image and the technique with which it was painted.

THE CREATION OF ADAM

The image of the hand of God that has just given the spark of life to Adam is one of the most suggestive in the whole cycle. Over the centuries it has become one of the symbols of the history of art of all time. The gentle female figure waiting in trepidation under the left arm of God could be Eve, not yet created but already present in the mind of the Creator.

THE FALL AND THE EXPULSION FROM PARADISE

The double scene was painted by Michelangelo at the end of the first stage of the decoration that concluded with the scene of the "Creation of Eve" and was unveiled in mid-August 1511. There was obviously a didactic intent in the comparison of the splendid pink-fleshed figure of Eve and the sombre, suddenly aged woman, who is sent away with Adam into a desolate land, having broken the divine commandment. The strong narrative content of this scene together with the force of dramatic feeling inevitably bring to mind the comparison with the same episodes painted by Masaccio nearly a century earlier in the Brancacci Chapel in the church of the Carmine in Florence.

The Deluge

This was the first element of the central section to be painted and one of the parts of the decoration where we can see clearly the hand of the assistants recorded in documents and who worked with Michelangelo only in the early stages of the work. In the centre of the background the ark can be seen as an architectural stricture coming out of the water; it is, in fact, a symbol of the Church representing the only possible salvation for man from sin. The tangle of nude figures in the centre of the scene recalls the lost cartoon for the "Battle of Cascina" painted by Michelangelo some years earlier.

THE PROPHET JOEL

The figures of Prophets and Sibyls are usually portrayed surrounded by animated "putti" representing angels or other spirits acting as intermediaries between man and God. The Prophet Joel is placed to left of the scene of the "Drunkness of Noah"; in the book of the Old Testament dedicated to Joel the destruction of the vines and harvest of Israel is foretold.

THE PROPHET ISAIAH

Vasari noted the beautiful expression of this figure, whose attention is caught by the "putto" at his shoulder. The crossed legs and heavy folds of the drapery give dynamic force to the form, while the right arm, crossing the figure, serves to define the space.

ESAIAS

The Libyan Sibyl

Vasari's enthusiasm for this figure seems thoroughly justified. In terms of form and movement it is, in fact, a brilliant creation: the dynamic pose of the turning figure, the iridescent colour of the flowing drapery are elements that must have inspired many painters of early Mannerism. Here there is a strong contrast between the sketchy, almost unfinished aspect of the two "putti" in the background and the elaborate, well-defined forms of the Sibyl.

IGNUDI WITH MEDALLION

The ten pairs of "Ignudi" sitting above the thrones of the Prophets hold festoons of oak leaves, a reference to the house of Della Rovere, the family of Julius II, and bronze medallions depicting stories from the Old Testament. Some of the figures are extraordinarily beautiful and probably supposed to represent angels, given their proximity to the scenes of the Holy stories. The figure to the left of the Delphic Sibyl has been almost completely lost as a result of an explosion that occurred in the powder room of the Castel Sant'Angelo in 1797. These figures have known extraordinary success in the history of painting; we only need cite the example of the ceiling of the Gallery of Palazzo Farnese in Rome, frescoed at the end of the Cinquecento by the Bolognese painter, Annibale Carracci (1560-1609), a leader of the classical tradition, whose figures are plainly inspired by Michelangelo's "Ignudi".

JUDITH AND HOLOFERNES (detail)

The two scenes painted in the pendentives above the entrance to the chapel are references to the salvation of the Hebrew people thanks to the heroism of David and Judith. The widow, Judith, does not hesitate to use her female skills to trick the Assyrian general, Holofernes, whose head she cuts off after having made him drunk. Michelangelo illustrates the moment following the dramatic act of heroism, with much attention to the detail of Judith's hair and drapery and the figure of the maidservant in the centre of the scene.

SPANDREL ABOVE THE LUNETTE WITH REHOBOAM

The biblical characters depicted in the eight spandrels of the vault exemplify the human condition before the coming of Christ. Within the family groups painted in these spaces the female figure appears to be of fundamental importance. The luminous transition of tone and the atmosphere of 'cosmic' serenity in this group recall the painting of Piero della Francesca.

below:
LUNETTE WITH ASA - JOSAPHAT - JORAM

In the fourteen lunettes of the walls are the Ancestors of Christ as listed at the beginning of the Gospel according to St. Matthew (I; 1,17). The names of the figures are written in elegant capitals on rectangular plates placed in the centre of the lunettes. In these scenes the paint is applied by Michelangelo in a fluent, almost summary way. In a manner similar to that used by the artist in sculpture, some of the background figures are barely sketched, creating at times a decidedly naturalistic effect. In this lunette, the splendid figure of the wise king Josaphat stands out. He is shown intent on his writing and wrapped in a great yellow-orange cloak; in his animated features we note the individual characteristics typical of a portrait.

THE LAST JUDGEMENT
13.70 x 12.20 m

To free the wall completely for the work, three frescoes by Perugino in the lower part were destroyed and Michelangelo himself did not hesitate to destroy the two lunettes painted at the same time as the ceiling.

Work started in November 1536 and the fresco was unveiled on 31 October 1541, twenty-nine years after the completion of the ceiling. In the two lunettes are angels with the symbols of Christ's Passion and immediately below the central corbel is the "statuesque" group of Christ, the judge, with the figure of the Madonna beside him. The central part is filled with those who have passed through the divine judgement: on the left the elected ascend to Heaven, on the right we witness the desperate fall of the damned, while

angels blow their trumpets in the centre. The lower part, just above the altar represents, on the left, the resurrection of the flesh and, on the right, the entrance to Hell.

Following a pronouncement of the Council of Trent of 3 December 1563, banning the representation of naked figures in places of worship, some of the "Ignudi" were subject to censorship and alterations were made just after the death of Michelangelo by his faithful follower, Daniele da Volterra, who, as is well known, was given the witty nickname of "brachettone" (breeches). Documents record many other works of repainting on the fresco, which in recent years appeared considerably darkened.

The cleaning was started in 1990 and was completed in 1994.

The Restoration of the Sistine Chapel Frescoes

The restoration of Michelangelo's frescoes in the Sistine Chapel represents the natural sequel to the work carried out between 1964 and 1974 on the fifteenth century "Histories of Moses and of Christ" on the side walls, and again between 1979 and 1980 on the sixteenth century repainting of the two biblical episodes on the entrance wall.

The cleaning of Michelangelo's ceiling was to have followed that of the series of portraits of the Popes, but the conditions noted in the lunette of "Eleazar Mathan" – in particular the presence of numerous micro-tears in the painted surface – advised against further delay, and between 1980 and 1984 the fourteen lunettes with the "Ancestor of Christ" were cleaned, together with the "Popes" by Perugino, Ghirlandaio, Botticelli and Cosimo Rosselli.

The damage proved to be the result of variations in temperature and humidity, causing contractions in the layer of glue which during past restorations had been applied to the painted surface as a varnish in order to revive the colours, darkened and dulled by the gradual build-up of deposits of dust and candle-black that the methods of cleaning generally used – bread, sour wine and water – were not able to sufficiently lighten.

The restoration revealed a pure colour, full of iridescent effects, and very similar to that brought to light by the careful restoration of the "Doni Tondo", also being carried out at that time. And yet it was unexpected, and consequently raised doubts and incredulity in some critics, causing the fierce polemic that for a time accompanied the work.

Following this first period of work, the cleaning of the ceiling itself took place between 1985 and 1989 and confirmed the results of the restoration of the lunettes. Finally, from the spring of 1990. work went ahead on the "Last Judgement", revealing yet again a rich source of new knowledge.

As we know, every restoration provides a rich and almost inexhaustible source of information about the functioning of the creative process and gives clues and solutions to problems of dating, iconography and style relating to the creation of the work of art. If this is true in general, it is all the more so in the case

of Michelangelo's frescoes, where the smoke, dust, dirt and restorations of nearly five centuries had deposited a patina, which, if not noble, was undoubtedly suggestive, giving rise to the myth of an artist who technically lacked preparation.

The cleaning of the ceiling has, however, revealed the work of a typical Renaissance artist, a sculptor by vocation, a reluctant painter and architect, with a technical background and artistic preparation that enabled him, despite his apparent inexperience, to tackle the most monumental challenge that an artist had ever faced, creating a work of exceptional skill both in terms of formal perfection and of technical achievement, the equivalent of a treatise on mural painting.

True to his Florentine origins, Michelangelo painted in "buon fresco", gradually eliminating from his palette – perhaps because of problems of 'mould' in the early stages – those colours like red lead that required the use of a binding medium. The use of "fresco secco" was limited to retouching and to the monochrome medallions at the feet of the "Ignudi". From the point of view of technique of execution, all the methods employed – in particular the use of enamel and lapislazuli in fresco – came from the workshop of Domenico Ghirlandaio, where Michelangelo served his apprenticeship, and from where he summoned most of the assistants who worked with him in the early stages of the work: Bugiardini, Jacopo di Sandro – with whom he immediately came into conflict – Jacopo di Lazzaro Torni known as Indaco Vecchio, who took the latter'place in January 1509, and his child-hood friend, Granacci, who had introduced him to the bottega of Ghirlandaio.

Michelangelo could certainly not have learnt, during the brief stay of these 'assistants' on the scaffolding, the difficult technique of painting in true fresco; they helded to 'freshen up' the knowledge assimilated during his apprenticeship with Ghirlandaio. They assisted in the layout of the work and painted not only the decorative elements of the cornices but also – under the rigid and constant control of the master – some of the figures of the stories of Noah. We note their presence in the different modes of painting and, often, in the sudden lowering of quality compared to the parts by Michelangelo which, even in the early stages, are of a constantly high level, unattainable by any other artist.

The assistants worked with him until the autumn of 1509 when the scale of the figures and the rhythms of the composition in the "Fall of Man" made it impossible for them to work with him on the scaffolding in any way that was even partially autonomous. So Michelangelo sent home the more able of his assistants – Granacci and Bugiardini in particular – above all because, according to the contract, all the expenses fell to him and there was no sense in keeping them if he could not put them to good use.

The decoration has also substantiated the fact, indicated by the chronicles and letters, that there was a pause in the work in the summer of 1510, immediately after Michelangelo had painted the "Creation of Eve", below which stood significantly the marble screen separating the laity from the clergy. It has also shown that once work started again in the autumn of 1511, the pace accelerated remarkably, so that, for example, the lunette of "Rehoboam and Abjijah" and the scene of the "Separation of light from darkness" were painted in one day. One reason for this acceleration was probably the use, in the scenes from Genesis in the centre of the ceiling and of the groups of figures in the spandrels, of the indirect impression, dispensing with the pouncing of the "spolvero" as used almost everywhere in the first series of frescoes.

As a result of the cleaning, the influence that Michelangelo had on his contemporaries becomes more than evident. It can be seen in Raphael and his entourage – particularly Giulio Romano – as well as in the so-called Florentine Mannerism of Rosso, Pontormo, Andrea del Sarto and Beccafumi, who were influenced not only in formal terms but also – and this was not noted before – by his use of colour.

It was a very different artist who painted the "Last Judgement" little more than twenty years later. Technically Michelangelo executed his composition in "buon fresco" as before on the ceiling, but here his palette is richer and, alongside the usual earth colours, we find pigments such as red lake, "giallolino" and orpiment. For the blue of the sky he freely used the very expensive lapislazuli, most probably chosen because here it was no longer the artist who bore the expense but the Pope. Apart from this detail the use of lapislazuli is fundamental, for it determines the generally much warmer tone, clearly a result of the artist's changing sensibility, influenced undoubtedly both by his familiarity over a period of twenty years with the work of Sebastiano del Piombo and by a journey to Venice made in 1529.

Although essentially Florentine by training, Michelangelo turned in his later works to new ideas that in terms of light and colour came from the Venetian School, showing his awareness of the outside world and his lack of prejudice towards a cultural environment about which, in words at least, he expressed many reservations.

Fabrizio Mancinelli

The Pauline Chapel

THE CONVERTION OF ST. PAUL
AND THE CRUCIFIXION OF ST. PETER
625 x 661 cm (each fresco)

In 1541 Michelangelo was commissioned to paint two frescoes in the Vatican Palace in Paul III's private chapel, built in 1537-40 by Antonio da Sangallo the Younger. The artist painted the "Conversion of St. Paul" (1542-45) and the "Crucifixion of St. Peter" (1546-50). The two great paintings are a conscious and coherent continuation of the formal and spiritual tendencies manifest in the "Last Judgement" in the Sistine Chapel. The foreshortened perspective, the truncated figures in the foreground, the cold, subdued tones of the palette, the total predominance of the human figure, abandoned in a desolate or rarefied, poetic landscape, are all characteristics that were to become typical of late Mannerist art in Rome. With the completion of these last great works of painting, achieved "with much effort", as the seventy-five year-old artist himself confessed to Vasari, Michelangelo appeared to be Masaccio reborn in Rome in the mid 16th century.

ROME

San Pietro in Vincoli

TOMB OF JULIUS II

Originally destined for the basilica of St. Peter in Vaticano, the monument was erected in the church of San Pietro in Vincoli in February 1545. Michelangelo's 'official' biographer, Ascanio Condivi, states in 1553 that it consists of a single facade placed against the wall, instead of the four planned in the original project. For the artist the commission came to represent a real tragedy – as Condivi himself calls it – which involved, among other things, the drawing up of five different contracts. Only the statues of "Moses", "Rachel" and "Leah" are by Michelangelo's own hand, while the rest is mainly the work of his assistants, notably Raffaello da Montelupo (1505- c.1566).

MOSES
Marble, ht. 235 cm

The statue was made between 1513-16, with some parts completed in the years 1542-45. It is a work of extraordinary power and expressivity, linked stylistically to the frescoes of the Prophets in the Sistine Chapel.

Condivi (1553) underlines the influence of antique sculptures, while Vasari (1568) gives a detailed and admiring description emphasizing the technical virtuosity in the hair and beard "that it seems that the chisel must have been exchanged for a brush".

THE CONTEMPLATIVE AND ACTIVE LIFE (LEAH AND RACHEL)
Marble, ht. 209 and 197 cm respectively

Made by Michelangelo in 1542 "in less than a year" (Vasari). Vasari
explicitly identifies the two figures with the biblical daughters of Laban,
Rachel and Leah, representing respectively the Contemplative and the
Active Life. The figure of Rachel is also a clear reference to the grie-
ving Virgin of the Pietà (c. 1515) by the Venetian painter, Sebastiano
del Piombo. in the Civic Museum in Viterbo – a painting that Michelangelo must have particularly admired because based on his conceptions
of painting.

Santa Maria sopra Minerva

THE RISEN CHRIST
Marble, ht. 205 cm

Michelangelo was commissioned to make the statue by Metello Vari and two other Roman gentlemen in 1514. A first version of the work, now lost, was rejected because a black vein appeared in the marble. The second version was made in Florence between the beginning of 1519 and April 1520. Some of the finishing touches were added by two of Michelangelo's assistants, Pietro Urbano and Federico Frizzi.

Piazza del Campidoglio

The redesigning of the Capitoline Hill was decided in 1537 by Pope Paul III, who had the square levelled and the famous statue of "Marcus Aurelius" moved there from the Lateran and placed on a base, specifically designed by Michelangelo, in the centre of the square. In the ten years 1544-54 work went ahead on the new façade for the Senate and the external staircase. The grand staircase is majestic and imposing but at the same time fluid and elegant thanks to the numerous mouldings; it is, in fact, the only part of the complex that we can say with certainty was planned and built by Michelangelo. Michelangelo's project for the whole complex has not survived but probably dates from 1560-61, following the election of Pope Pius IV (Giovanni Angelo de' Medici, 1499-1565), who gave a vital impulse to the works. We have, however, a fairly clear idea of Michelangelo's intentions from two engravings of 1569 and 1575 by Etienne Dupérac. Another engraving by the same Parisian artist, dating from 1567 and featuring the plan of the square, has been used, particularly, as the basis for the repaving of the square according to Michelangelo's design, carried out in 1940. The beautiful Palazzo dei Conservatori was finished (1564-76) under the direction of Giacomo della Porta, essentially in the way indicated by Michelangelo, whereas the twin building of Palazzo Nuovo or dei Musei was built from 1603 to 1654 by the Roman architect, Gerolamo Rainaldi (1570-1655).

Porta Pia

According to Vasari (1568) Michelangelo was commissioned by Pius IV to make a plan for the construction of a new monumental gateway, called Pia in his honour; the artist "made three, all wonderfully beautiful". A contract for the construction of the gate was, in fact, drawn up on 2 July 1561 giving Michelangelo the commission to direct the undertaking.

Payments were already made in 1561 to the architect, Pier Luigi Gaeta, who must have taken charge of the works for Michelangelo. Other payments, made in May 1562 for the Pope's great Medici coat of arms above the pediment and the fine mask in the centre of the architrave, refer to the Sicilian sculptor and architect, Jacopo del Duca (c.1520-c.1601), who had worked with Michelangelo on other occasions. The central crowning in neo-classical style was added between 1861 and 1864 by the architect, Virginio Vespignani. Michelangelo's emphasis on the central gateway is confirmed by studies made by the artist on this theme. The elegant side windows and the – more delicate – blind upper windows give the whole ensemble a decorative note that some scholars have interpreted as pre-Baroque.

Siena
Cathedral

Piccolomini Altar
right:
St. Peter, St. Paul
Marble, ht. 124, 127 cm respectively

Monsignor Francesco Todeschini Piccolomini, a nephew of Pius II, commissioned the
altar from the Lombard sculptor, Andrea Breg-
no, who worked on it with his assistants from
1481 to 1485.
On 19 June 1501, Michelangelo signed a contract to make fifteen sculptures and complete
the statue of St. Francis, already started by the
sculptor, Pietro Torrigiani (1472-1528), better
known for having broken Michelangelo's nose
with his fist. Michelangelo must have worked
on the four statues actually produced between
the spring of 1503 and the late summer of
1504. In these sculptures, maybe because of
their more modest dimensions that were less
congenial to the artist, Michelangelo's work
appears, for once, to lack that aura of unap-
proachable "terribilità" that even to the eye
of the modern observer seems to surround his
art. Stylistically the works are linked to the
"Pietà" in the Vatican, the "David" in the
Accademia in Florence and most of all to the
Bruges "Madonna", which some critics consider to have been made originally for the Piccolomini Altar. The statue of "St. Paul" appears
to be of a higher quality; in the saint's face we
most probably see a self-portrait of the artist
before his profile was altered by the famous
Torrigiani fist.

BOLOGNA
San Domenico

ST. PETRONIUS, ST. PROCULUS,
ANGEL HOLDING A CANDELABRUM
Marble, ht. 64, 58.5 and 51.5 cm respectively

The three statues were commissioned in 1494
by Giovanfrancesco Aldovrandi, a member of
the government of the city, who had become
friends with Michelangelo during his stay
in Bologna, lasting about one year. The
sculptures fit harmoniously into the complex
monument begun by Fra Guglielmo from
Pisa in 1267, following a project by Nicola
Pisano, and completed two centuries later
with the cornice (1469-73) added by the
sculptor, Niccolò dell'Arca (c. 1435-1494)
from Puglia. Stimulated by this history,
Michelangelo develops the extraordinary
interpretative relationship with the artistic
culture of the past that characterizes his
early work. The most interesting sculpture is
perhaps "St. Proculus", whose attribution to
Michelangelo was long debated by scholars
because the work is not specifically mentioned with the others by Condivi or Vasari.
The burning frown of the young saint – in
whose face some have seen the self-portrait
of the nineteen year-old Buonarroti – is a
precious anticipation of that of the colossus
in the Galleria dell'Accademia in Florence.
The figure of "St. Petronius" is a reference
to early fifteenth century sculpture from
Donatello to Jacopo della Quercia, and the
"Angel holding a Candelabrum", with its
softly modelled forms, brings to mind the
delicate classical purity of Luca della Robbia.

MILANO
Castello Sforzesco

RONDANINI PIETÀ
Marble, ht. 195 cm

In a letter to the artist's nephew, Leonardo Buonarroti, Michelangelo's faithful disciple, Daniele da Volterra (c.1509-1566) writes that the artist worked assiduously on this sculpture until six days before his death on 18 February 1564. Michelangelo started work on the sculpture at the end of 1556, having abandoned the Florentine "Pietà", making two different versions; the legs of Christ and the separated right arm, in fact, belong to the first version. The artist left the work to his apprentice, Antonio del Franzese. It is not known when the "Pietà" was moved to the Palazzo Rondanini in Rome. In 1952 it was purchased by Count Sanseverino for the city of Milan and placed in its present location. It seems almost superfluous to underline the extraordinary power of suggestion and pathos that emanates from these holy figures, never before made so tragically human.

PARIS

Louvre

DYING SLAVE AND REBELLIOUS SLAVE
Marble, ht. 229 and 215 cm respectively

The two sculptures were made in 1514-16, just after the "Moses" in the church of San Pietro in Vincoli in Rome, for the tomb of Julius II. As it was not possible to include them in the much reduced version of the project, Michelangelo gave them to Roberto Strozzi, who in turn presented them to King Henri II of France. They at one time belonged to Cardinal Richelieu (1632) before becoming the property of the State and being moved to the Louvre in 1794. Vasari (1568) suggests a 'political' interpretation of the Slaves for the tomb of Julius II – he sees them as representing the provinces brought back under the jurisdiction of Church by the Pope – while Condivi (1553) suggests they were the personification of the Liberal Arts, definitively suppressed with the death of the Pope. The antique prototypes may have been the statues of Marsyas, dating from the Hellenistic period, although authoritative scholars of Michelangelo's work have underlined the metahistorical and universal fascination of the works. With its primigenial force, the "Rebellious Slave" is closer to the Slaves in the Accademia in Florence, while the "Dying Slave" is characterized by an indescribable sense of exhaustion and languor.

BRUGES
Notre-Dame

MADONNA AND CHILD
Marble, ht. 128 cm

This statue, made in about 1504, probably for the Piccolomini Altar in Siena Cathedral, was taken to Bruges in 1506 by Francesco Del Pugliese and purchased by the merchant, Alexander Mouscron. However, the precise identification of this work is uncertain because both Condivi (1553) and Vasari (1568) refer to a sculpture in bronze. It is mentioned for the first time in the "Diary of a Journey" (1521) by the great German Renaissance artist, Albrecht Dürer. In the alabaster-like purity of her face and the working of the veil the Madonna is very close to the Madonna of the "Pietà" in the Vatican.

LONDON

Royal Academy

National Gallery

MADONNA AND CHILD WITH ST. JOHN
("TADDEI TONDO")
Marble, ht. 109 cm

THE ENTOMBMENT
Painting on panel, 161 x 149 cm

The relief is described by Vasari (1568) when it was still in the house of the Florentine purchaser, Taddeo Taddei. It was sold in Rome in 1823 to Sir George Beaumont and has been in the Royal Academy since 1830. It pro-dates the "Pitti Tondo" in the Bargello National Museum in Florence.

First mentioned, with reference to Michelangelo, in a Roman inventory, made in 1967, of the possessions of the Farnese family, the work was in the Fesch Collection in Rome in the 19th century and than in that of the English painter, Macpherson, who in 1868 sold it to the National Gallery. The largely unfinished work was cleaned in 1968-9.
The most probable identification of the

figures is as follows: from left to right, Mary Magdalene, Nicodemus, Christ held from behind by Joseph of Arimathaea, St. John (for a long time confused with the figure of the Magdalene), the outline of the Virgin Mary on the ground and, behind, Mary Salome or Mary, the sister of Martha. Despite the unfinished state of the work, it is the only painting that can be stylistically compared to the "Doni Tondo" in the Uffizi. The work was possibly started in 1506 and destined for the chapel that Michelangelo planned in the first project for the tomb of Julius II or, according to another hypothesis, it may be the painting started by the artist in 1501 for the Augustinian fathers in Rome.

Essential bibliography

G. VASARI, *La vita di Michelangelo nelle redazioni del 1550 e del 1568*, edited by P. Barocchi, vol. I, Milan-Naples, 1962.

A. CONDIVI, *Vita di Michelangelo Buonarroti*, Rome, 1553; edited by P. d'Ancona, Milan, 1928.

C. DE TOLNAY, *Michelangelo*, I-V, Princeton, N.J., 1943-1960.

P. BAROCCHI, *Michelangelo e la sua scuola: i disegni di Casa Buonarroti e degli Uffizi*, Firenze, 1962.

AA.VV., *Michelangelo architetto*, a cura di P. Portoghesi e B. Zevi, Turin, 1964.

P. BAROCCHI-R. RISTORI, *Il Carteggio di Michelangelo*, I-IV, Firenze, 1965-1979.

L. GOLDSCHEIDER, *Michelangelo*, London-New York. 1967.

C. DE TOLNAY, *Corpus dei disegni di Michelangelo*. I-IV, Novara, 1971-1980.

AA.VV., *La Cappella Sistina. I primi restauri: la scoperta del colore*, Novara, 1986.

F. MANCINELLI, *Il cantiere di Michelangelo per la volta della Cappella Sistina*, in "La pittura in Italia. Il Cinquecento", tomo II, Milan, 1988, pp. 535-552.

AA.VV., *La Cappella Sistina. La volta restaurata: il trionfo del colore*, Novara, 1992.

ATS Italia Editrice s.r.l.
Via di Brava, 41/43 – 00163 Roma
www.atsitalia.it

Photographs:
Archive ATS Italia Editrice
Vatican Museums Photographic Archive
Photographic Archive Scala
"Madonna and Child with St. John" © Royal Academy of Arts, London
"The Entombment" © National Gallery, London

The images of the Scala Archive which reproduce cultural heritage belonging to the Italian State are published courtesy of the Ministry of National Heritage and Culture.

The editor is at disposal of all those who lay claims to unfound iconographic sources.

Graphic project, paging and cover: ATS Italia Editrice

Chromatic scanning and corrections: ATS Italia Editrice (Ilaria Ratti)

Printing: Kina Italia/L.E.G.O. - Italy

ISBN 88-87654-63-8